EXPRESSIVE AND RECEPTIVE FINGERSPELLING FOR HEARING ADULTS

LaVera M. Guillory

Baton Rouge
CLAITOR'S PUBLISHING DIVISION

Library of Congress Catalog Card Number
66-17803

14th reprint, 1999

Published and for sale by
CLAITOR'S PUBLISHING DIVISION
3165 S. Acadian at I-10, P.O. Box 261333
Baton Rouge, LA 70826-1333
Tel: 800-274-1403 (In LA 225-344-0476)
Fax: 225-344-0480

Internet address:
e mail: claitors@claitors.com
World Wide Web: http://www.claitors.com

To JOHN and MARGARET

Whose pride, interest and cooperation

made it possible for their mother to be a teacher also.

ACKNOWLEDGMENTS

Dr. Lloyd V. Funchess, Superintendent, and Mr. Edward L. Scouten, Principal, of the Louisiana School for the Deaf – for their encouragement and interest in the development of the idea for this method of fingerspelling.

Dr. William J. McClure, Superintendent of the Indiana School for the Deaf, whose interest was the incentive for organizing the material into book form in preparation for publication.

Mrs. Virginia Boles, teacher at the Louisiana School for the Deaf – an invaluable "sounding board" and good listener whose keen insight, questions and suggestions helped develop the idea for this method for fingerspelling, who offered moral support and assistance that contributed to the success of the first experimental class.

PREFACE

The introduction of the Rochester Method of Instruction by Edward L. Scouten, Principal of the Louisiana State School for the Deaf, created new interest in fingerspelling. Young in-service teachers were learning dactylology, and it also became apparent that many of us with years of teaching experience could use some improvement in the art. This situation prompted the development of the material contained in this collection.

Although it was designed for use in teaching a class in fingerspelling, the material, in its present form, is not meant to be an exact lesson plan. It is merely the projection of an idea and a collection of drill material with a few suggestions for its use.

If this preliminary effort proves to be worthwhile and helpful to others, it is the author's hope to complete the project in book form.

FOREWORD

Fingerspelling, or dactylology, is not a new form of communication, but it occurred to the writer that there might be a new and more meaningful method of gaining skill in the art. Since the beginner in dactylology might be compared to the young child learning to read and write, might not the method used for his instruction be applicable to fingerspelling?

Could we not use phonetics in learning to fingerspell instead of memorizing the hand positions of individual letters? This question prompted the assimilation of the material contained in this booklet. It is a plan for learning to fingerspell basic phonetic elements found in the English language instead of learning the individual letters of the manual alphabet.

TABLE OF CONTENTS

Page

INTRODUCTION 1

COMMON FAULTS IN FINGERSPELLING 3

NOTES FOR THE TEACHER OF FINGERSPELLING 5

THE FIRST LESSON AND INTRODUCTION TO PHONETICAL FINGERSPELLING 7

HINTS FOR EXPRESSIVE FINGERSPELLING 9

READING FINGERSPELLED WORDS AND SENTENCES 11

THE USE OF PHONETIC COMBINATIONS 14

BASIC PHONETIC ELEMENTS IN THREE-LETTER RHYMING WORDS 15

DRILLS FOR THREE-LETTER WORDS 23

PRACTICE IN SENTENCE FORM 25

DRILLS FOR FOUR-LETTER WORDS 26

COMMONLY USED WORDS 29

COMPLIMENTARY OR COURTESIES 30

LONGER WORDS 32

DIGRAPHS 35

PREFIXES AND SUFFIXES 37

SYLLABICATION 38

THE AMERICAN MANUAL ALPHABET 41

THE AMERICAN MANUAL NUMBERS 43

INTRODUCTION

Since this material was developed specifically for teaching adult hearing persons to fingerspell, it is taken for granted that the adult hears, speaks and also has fully developed reading and writing skills. However, it might be of interest to know that during its origin the method was experimentally used to teach an illiterate, seventy-year-old person, who in ten or fifteen minutes, learned to fingerspell and recognize several words in the an, can, ran series.

An old and common approach to fingerspelling was that the interested hearing person obtained a manual alphabet card, from which he learned the twenty-six different hand positions that represent the letters of the alphabet. Then he set about spelling out words letter by letter.

With constant practice this person eventually learned to spell and see words, but, in many instances, others using this method continued to spell out each word and to see only letters, never whole words, when reading fingerspelling. Even after becoming quite skilled in the action of forming the letters and in recognizing those letters they saw, many apparently either did not realize they were expected to see words or if they did, failed to break the old habit of spelling and reading letter by letter.

The hearing "letter-reading" teacher must be a source of constant frustration to the deaf pupil, especially the older pupil who has a large vocabulary. What emotional strain must be experienced when a pupil, required to give answers in fingerspelling, must spell each letter individually in order that the teacher can recognize each letter of each word! To analogize, the situation might be comparable to a hearing person forced to spell letter by letter instead of speaking words, to a skilled typist forced to type letter by letter, or someone accustomed to write as fast as he can think forced to decrease his speed to a slow, deliberate pace, carefully forming each letter of every word. Another analogy is a class with the hearing teacher spelling to her hearing pupils, and they, in turn, spelling every answer or thought expressed in a class discussion.

Two factors in fingerspelling are quite obvious – first, the physical actions of expressing an idea and second, the visual action of receiving one. In using the Rochester Method, a third factor is involved. We must be constantly aware that the fingerspelling is used only to supplement speech and lipreading. Therefore, we must speak or silently form every word on the lips at the same instant it is spelled. The phonetic sound necessary for lipreading must appear on the lips and the hand at the same instant.

The first rule of fingerspelling and speaking words simultaneously might be <u>to let the fingers set the pace for speech</u>. To do this, it is necessary to form the habit of thinking longer words in syllables.

COMMON FAULTS IN FINGERSPELLING

Some of the common faults in fingerspelling are mentioned here so that they may be avoided by the beginner. If fingerspelling is to be used as a means of teaching speech and English to the deaf, it must be used correctly. The teacher must quickly learn to fingerspell whole words – not individual letters. The reason for this may be better understood if one stops to consider the fact that the deaf child "hears" only what he sees.

Now, consider the effect of the letter-spelling fingerspeller on her deaf lipreading pupil. One common mistake is made by a teacher who fails to match the speed of her speech to the speed of her fingerspelling. Consequently, she spells only the key words in the sentence. Please note, she spells these key words letter by letter. Since it is impossible to think the letters for the fingerspelled word and say the whole word at the same time, her oral request, as she fingerspells, would sound like this, "P-u-t the b-o-o-k on the t-a-b-l-e." The deaf child sees on the fingers only three fingerspelled words: put, book, table. On the lips he sees only three words: the, on, the. The words p-u-t, b-o-o-k, and t-a-b-l-e, being enunciated aloud as letters while they are fingerspelled, are indistinct and meaningless to the lipreader.

A second type of letter-spelling fingerspeller might be one who fingerspells while silently thinking the letters, then says the word aloud. Her request would be: P-U-T (lips closed, fingerspelling) put (aloud) T-H-E (lips closed, fingerspelling) the (aloud) B-O-O-K (lips closed, fingerspelling) book (aloud) O-N (lips closed, fingerspelling) on (aloud) T-H-E (lips closed, fingerspelling) the (aloud) T-A-B-L-E (lips closed, fingerspelling) table (aloud). The deaf pupil sees first the fingerspelled word followed by the lips repeating the same word. If he were able to follow both, it might be called "echo talk."

Thus we see the importance of simultaneity in the lip and hand formation. With perfection, it is said, the deaf child actually has an illusion of speech and hearing.

NOTES FOR THE TEACHER OF FINGERSPELLING

The presentation of this material should be based on the skill of the individual members of the class. The ideal situation would be to have the whole class on one level. The material was written with the beginner in mind, but the class may vary from the beginner with no knowledge of fingerspelling to the professional interested in seeing how the method works.

A preliminary study of the material will enable the teacher to formulate his own plans for presentation.

It was originally planned for eight one-hour sessions, held twice weekly. This proved to be enough time for the intermediate pupils in the class (those already familiar with the formation of the alphabet but still spelling letters instead of words.) The beginners needed more practice sessions.

Following are a few points that might be helpful.

1. The first period should be used for explanation, motivation, etc., and a demonstration followed by a short practice session.
2. The succeeding class periods may be divided into about 10 minutes of discussion and 10 minutes for giving out new material and demonstrations -- 30 minutes for small group practice and about 10 minutes for final discussion and assignments for practice.
3. It is recommended that pupils divide their outside practice into several short periods rather than one long session.
4. Special attention needs to be given to most beginners to see that they are holding their hands correctly. This is one of the points that needs demonstration before the first practice session. It is one of the questions most often asked. A relaxed position should be explained and demonstrated.
5. At the first meetings – for practice – two or three beginners may be grouped with the more experienced who may give them help.

6. At subsequent meetings, the more experienced fingerspellers may begin to work together. They will move ahead more rapidly than the beginners. The beginners are able to work in larger groups as they progress and gain in confidence.
7. A brief explanation of the formation of the letter can be helpful if the letter is not being formed clearly.
8. Alphabet cards can be distributed after the first two or three classes to be used as reference for the correct hand positions. However, it should be stressed that the learner is not to study the hand positions in alphabetical sequence.
9. For a large class, an instructor should plan to have several assistants, skilled in dactylology. Their help is needed in working with small groups.

THE FIRST LESSON AND INTRODUCTION TO PHONETICAL FINGERSPELLING

Perfection in the use of the manual alphabet is the ability to express and receive ideas in fingerspelling as fluently as one reads or writes with a pen. Fingerspelling might be considered a form of writing without the use of pen and paper.

Let us consider the physical action of handwriting. Is each word spelled out or does the writer think and write words? Most adults write shorter and familiar words without thought of letters. Longer and unfamiliar words may be thought and simultaneously written as syllables. Why not use this same method when learning to fingerspell? Why not learn the manual alphabet in phonetic combinations instead of the formerly accepted alphabetical sequence?

A person interested in learning to fingerspell would do well to assess his reading ability. As the eyes glide across the sentences of this page, it can be noted that one sees words, phrases, or, perhaps, even whole sentences, depending upon the reader's skill. Each word is a separate and distinct picture made up of letters. Certainly a good reader gives no thought to the separate letters in each word but instantly recognizes the whole configuration or word. This is the same ability we seek to develop in reading fingerspelled words.

Where fingerspelling is learned in groups of letters to express the basic phonetics in a word, it is not difficult to fingerspell and, at the same time, say a word or syllable containing up to three or four letters. In practice, three or four letters in a syllable or word are all that are ever required of a fingerspeller, regardless of the length of the sentence or the word. This may be illustrated to a class by placing the following sentence on a chalkboard.

Chemical decomposition by the action of the electric current is called electrolysis.

To a beginner it may appear impossible to fingerspell and simultaneously speak the words of this sentence. Let us consider that the longer words can be spelled and spoken as syllables, but expressed on the hand without a break between syllables; thus appearing as a whole word. Now, mark the syllables:

Chem/i/cal de/com/po/si/tion by the ac/tion of the e/lec/tric cur/rent is call/ed e/lec/tro/ly/sis.

Demonstrate the fingerspelling and simultaneous speech.

Elaborate by giving other examples as needed.

Now present the first group of basic phonetic elements in rhyming three letter words.

Demonstrate and stress that the learner must speak the word simultaneously as he forms it on the hand.

HINTS FOR EXPRESSIVE FINGERSPELLING

1. Find a comfortable, easy position so that the hand can be relaxed.
   (a) Elbow down toward waist
   (b) Hand palm side out in a comfortable position about 6 or 8 inches beneath the chin. The hand is turned slightly at an angle with thumb side near the body.
2. The hand should be near enough to the lips for a deaf person to read the lips and get the action of the hand through the peripheral vision. Be careful that the hand never obstructs the view of the lips.
3. Develop a rhythmic style of fingerspelling that will show the break between words. However, it is not necessary to make a distinct break at the end of every word, since the accompanying lip movement clearly shows the break. (This is why we can read fingerspelled sentences with much greater ease if they are accompanied with a sound or, at least, a silent lip formation of the word.)

The following are a series of notes regarding fingerspelling. They were prepared by the late Dr. Zenas Freeman Westervelt and are published in a booklet by Edward L. Scouten entitled A Revaluation of the Rochester Method.

1. It is better for a teacher to spell no more rapidly than she can spell distinctly and with expression; whatever is faster than this is a disadvantage rather than a help.
2. Spelled words should attract and hold attention and interest, because of their clearness and intelligibility.
3. One proficient in dactylology is not in the habit of keeping his eye upon the hand of the speller, but watches the play of expression upon his face while, at the same time, the eye takes in the spelled language.
4. In teaching the little beginning child the spelled word we will not spell it slowly so that he recognizes and has time to consider the position taken by the hand for each letter, but the word is spelled so rapidly that all the little child can see is the general form of the word, the positions of the hand at the beginning of it, the duration of the movement and the

position at the end. In this way the child takes the word as a whole, and when the little child begins to realize that thought is conveyed in this way, he may put up his hand and give it a wriggle and then points to what he wants.

5. The usual rate of utterance of spelled language in class exercises is generally not over 80 to 100 words per minute. The rate of spelling in a chapel talk is from 100 to 125 words per minute.

6. In all class recitations two pupils answer questions simultaneously; one recites by manual spelling for the class to see, while the other, acting as his second, reads aloud from his hand, so that the teacher has a double answer to every question. This enables the teacher to correct the speech of the pupils, and also enables all the pupils to follow the recitation with greater precision than they could in an oral exercise, which lacks this manual accompaniment.

7. All new subject matter, all study of languages other than English, all study of technical subjects such as chemistry, philosophy, etc., all subjects which require great exactness of language utterance and understanding should be conducted through manual spelling from the beginning to the end of the school course.

READING FINGERSPELLED WORDS AND SENTENCES

There are many obvious reasons why it is easier for an adult to learn to fingerspell than it is to read fingerspelling. Probably the basic reason is that in fingerspelling we are transmitting a thought formed in our own mind -- a mental action followed by the physical. We set our own pace, slowing, repeating, starting over at will. In receiving another's idea, our thinking process is reversed and the mental action follows the physical.

A second reason is that we have many more opportunities for practice in the activity of fingerspelling. Therefore, from the very first, it would be wise to concentrate on methods to perfect the more passive reading skill.

Following is a list of suggestions:

1. When two or more people practice together, each may watch the formation of the word on the hand of the other, thereby memorizing the picture of the word as well as the feel of it.
2. When practicing alone, one can use a mirror to get a better view of the word. (Since the palm side of the hand is turned outward in fingerspelling the mirror image will give a better view for memorizing the appearance of a word).
3. A teacher of older pupils gets practice in her classroom. Pupils are most cooperative and helpful when encouraged to feel they are "teaching the teacher." (Actually it is also an incentive for them to use fingerspelling and give more thought to good English.)
4. The very best practice can be obtained through conversation with deaf adults. Their patience and kindness often seem to be endless; their command of syntax makes for easier reading.

5. Whenever the opportunity presents itself, concentrate on a good interpreter's hand and listen to the words being spoken.
6. Insist that the deaf fingerspeller use his voice or, at least, form the words on his lips. If the deaf person will do this, the vision of the word on his lips or the sound will make the break between the fingerspelled words for the hearing person as he uses his peripheral vision for the fingerspelling.
7. Context is important. Some words look very similar (especially when they begin and end in the same letters and contain the same number of letters.)

   For example: cab, cub.

   1. The____cried for its mother.
   2. The____driver was late.

   barn, born.

   1. The____was red.
   2. The child was____in July.

   vile, vale.

   1. We walked across the____.
   2. It was____weather.

8. If one loses a word, the remainder of the sentence may give a clue.

   1. Mary b--g-t a new dress.
   2. My sister is c-----g to visit.
   3. I got a doll for C-----t--s.
   4. I have two b--th--s and two sisters.

9. It might be helpful to realize that variations in fingerspelling comparable to differences in penmanship will be noted. Just as one person's handwriting may be more legible than another's, so one person's fingerspelling may be easier to read than another's. (For this

reason, one should strive for good "penmanship" in fingerspelling. Remember it is much easier to form good habits in the beginning than to break bad ones later.)

THE USE OF PHONETIC COMBINATIONS

The configurations shown on the succeeding pages were designed to be used in learning the basic phonetic elements of words. For their utilization, one must understand that they are to be used for the development of the ability to fingerspell words.

For illustration, take the word an. In writing this word with pen or pencil, one would think an, not the individual letters, a-n. In fingerspelling, one should be trained to follow the same method of thinking the whole word an, and the letters a-n are formed on the hand. After it has become automatic to think the word while spelling out the letters, one can precede an by the letter b. The formation becomes b-a-n, but the thought must be ban. When the word ban becomes routine, a new word can be formed by substituting the letter c for the b to form the word can. The same procedure can be followed through the family of words -- fan, man, pan, ran, tan, van.

After the first family of words has been mastered, it becomes successively easier to master the others.

Much concentration and practice plus determination and a true desire to learn will speed the learning process. Who could have more motivation for learning than a hearing person vitally interested in the deaf? It is a physical impossibility for some deaf persons to learn to speak our language perfectly. We must learn to use their medium.

BASIC PHONETIC ELEMENTS IN THREE-LETTER RHYMING WORDS

ab

ad

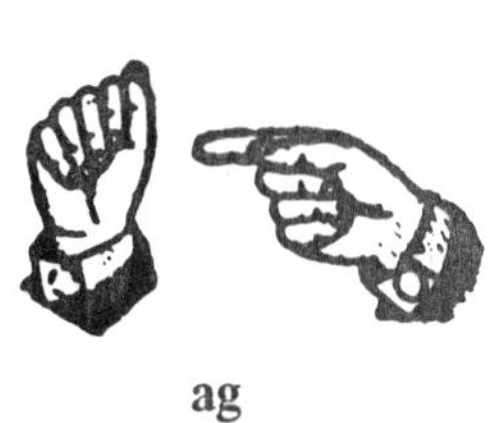
ag

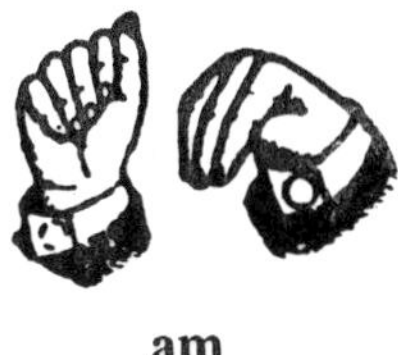
am

an

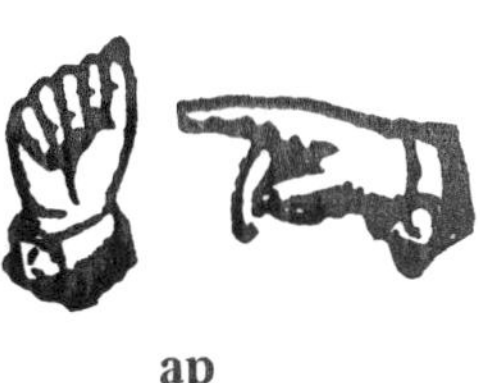
ap

ar

as

at

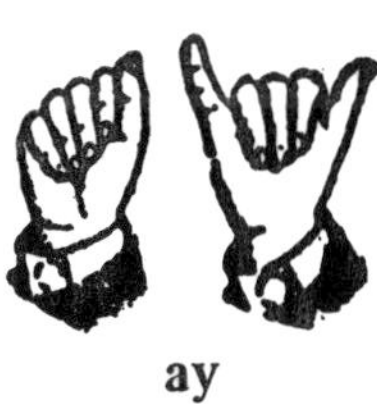
ay

ax

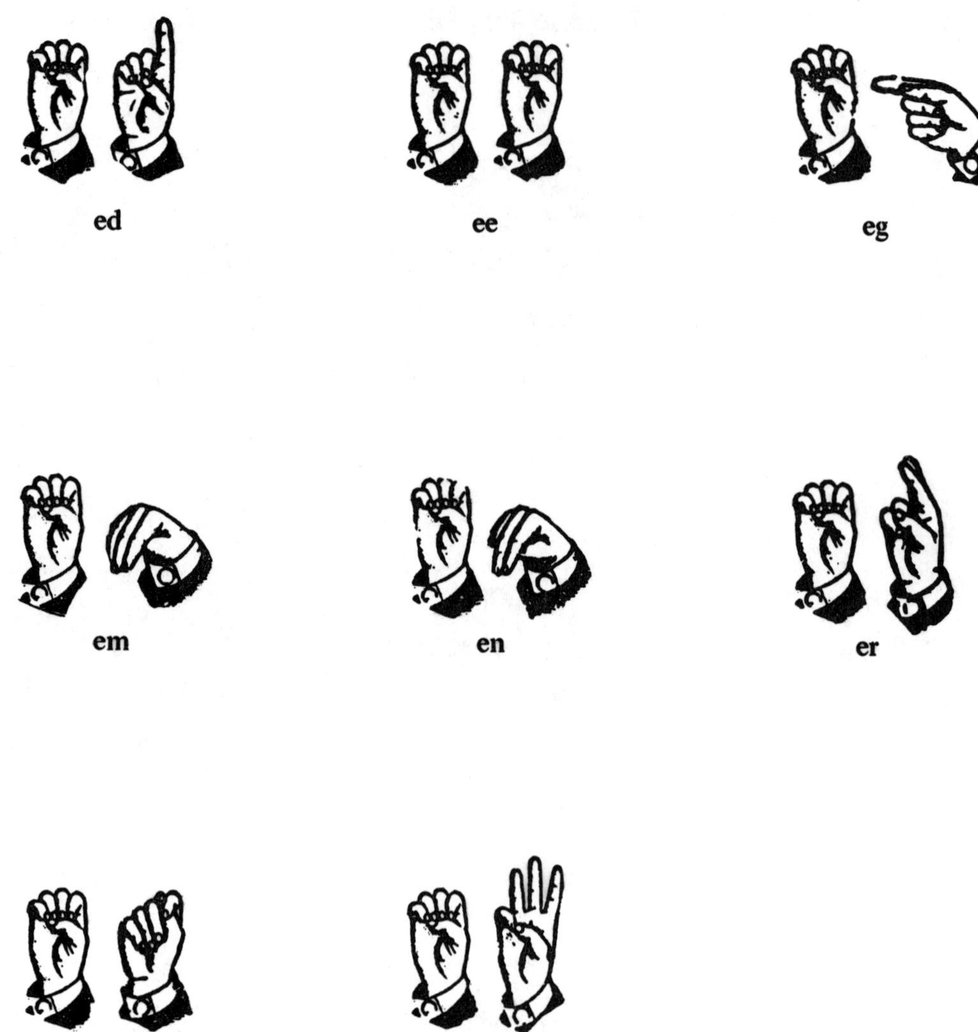
ed
ee
eg
em
en
er
et
ew

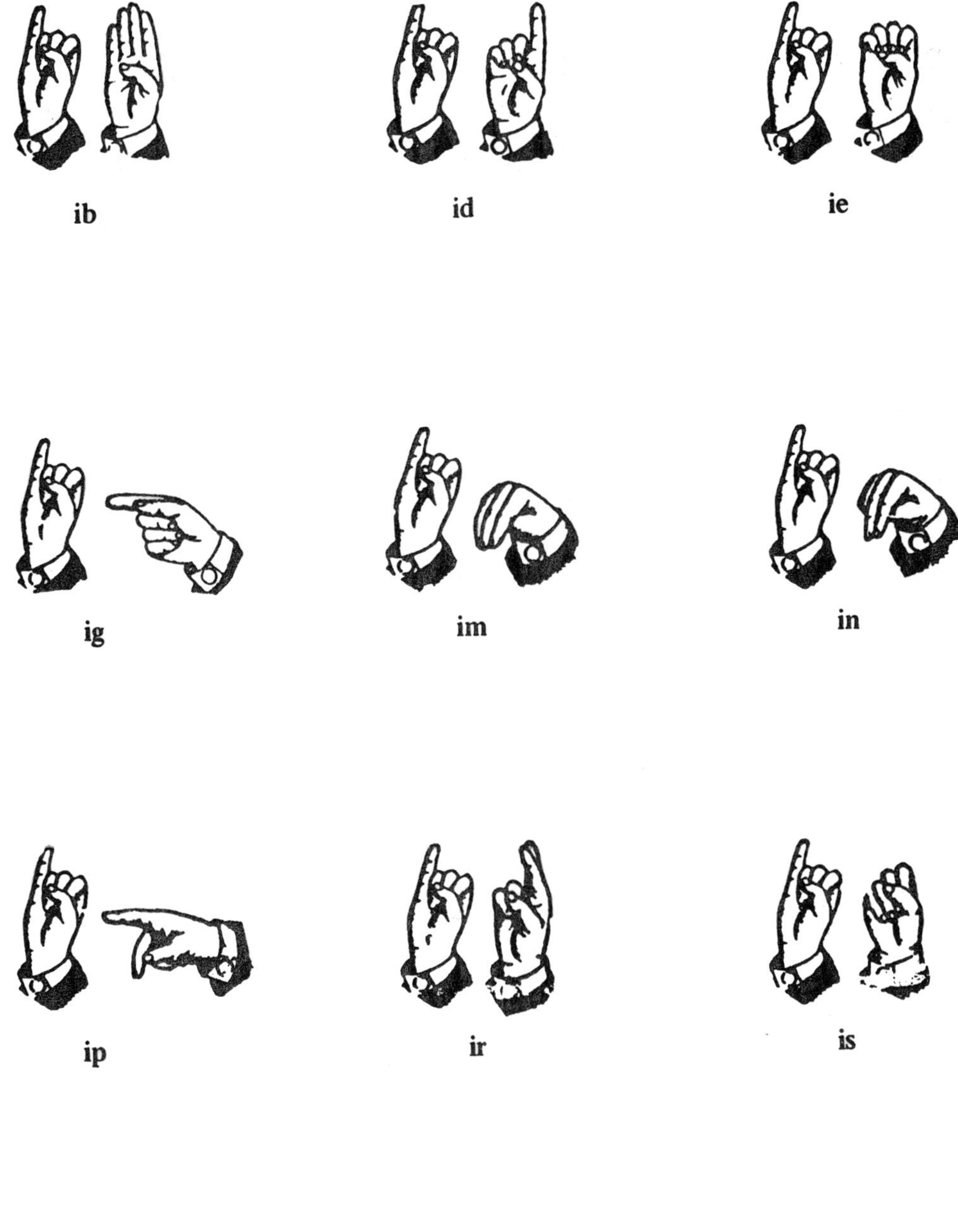

it

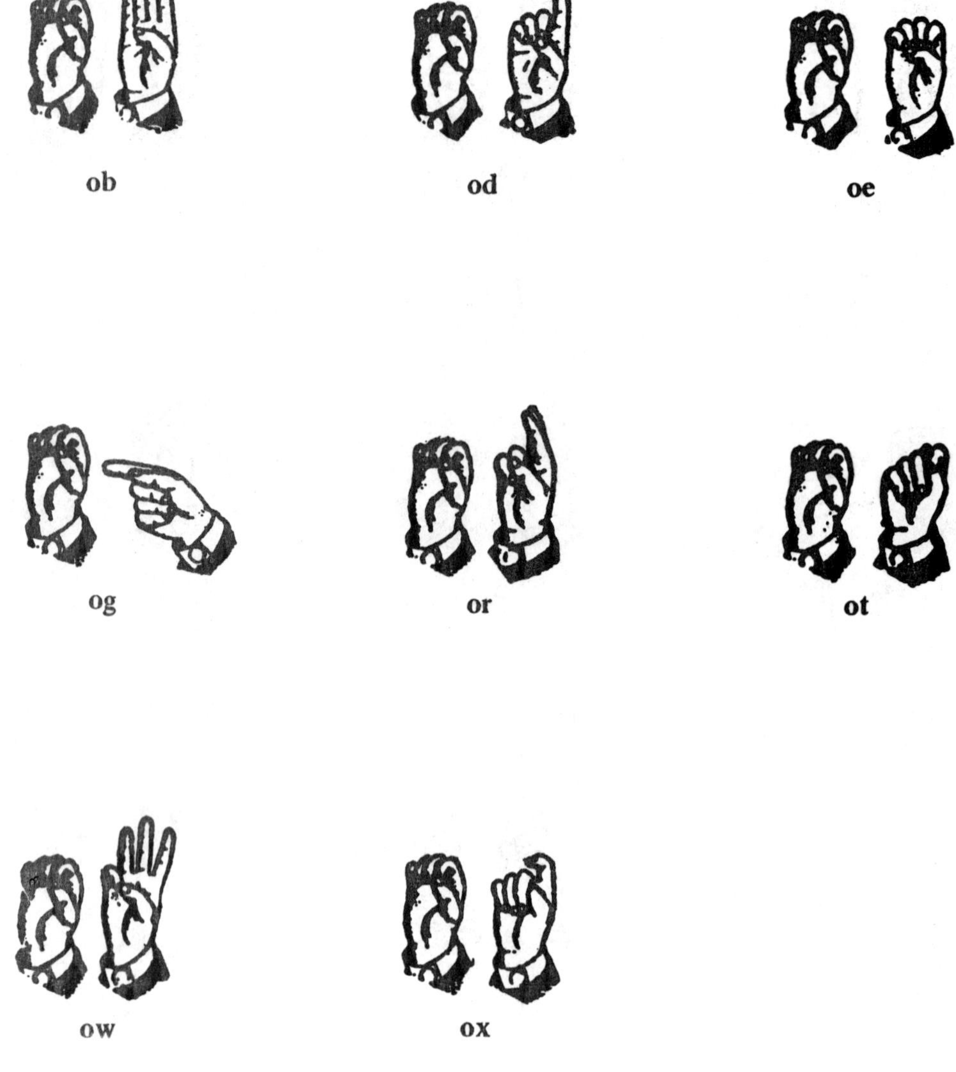
ob
od
oe
og
or
ot
ow
ox

ub

ud

ue

ug

um

un

up

ur

us

ut

The following hand formations have not been introduced in the preceding lessons. Care should be used to present their use as a symbol of sound, not as letters. For that reason, they are introduced now as one lesson to complete the presentation of all elements.

Since this is also the introduction to forming three-letter words from the basic phonetic elements, we point out that the words presented here are formed by combining those basic elements with a new formation. In the case of rhyming words, as used here, the basic element is preceded by the new formation.

For example: ab becomes cab, en becomes cen, og becomes fog, etc.

In presenting the new formations, care should be used to present their use as symbols of sounds and not as letters. For example: the c symbol will be introduced as the soft or hard c with the s or k sound. Say kab when demonstrating cab, and sen when demonstrating cen, pointing out that both ab and en are preceded by the same symbol to form the new words.

Emphasize: Concentrate on saying the word, thinking the word, and seeing the word. NEVER LETTERS!

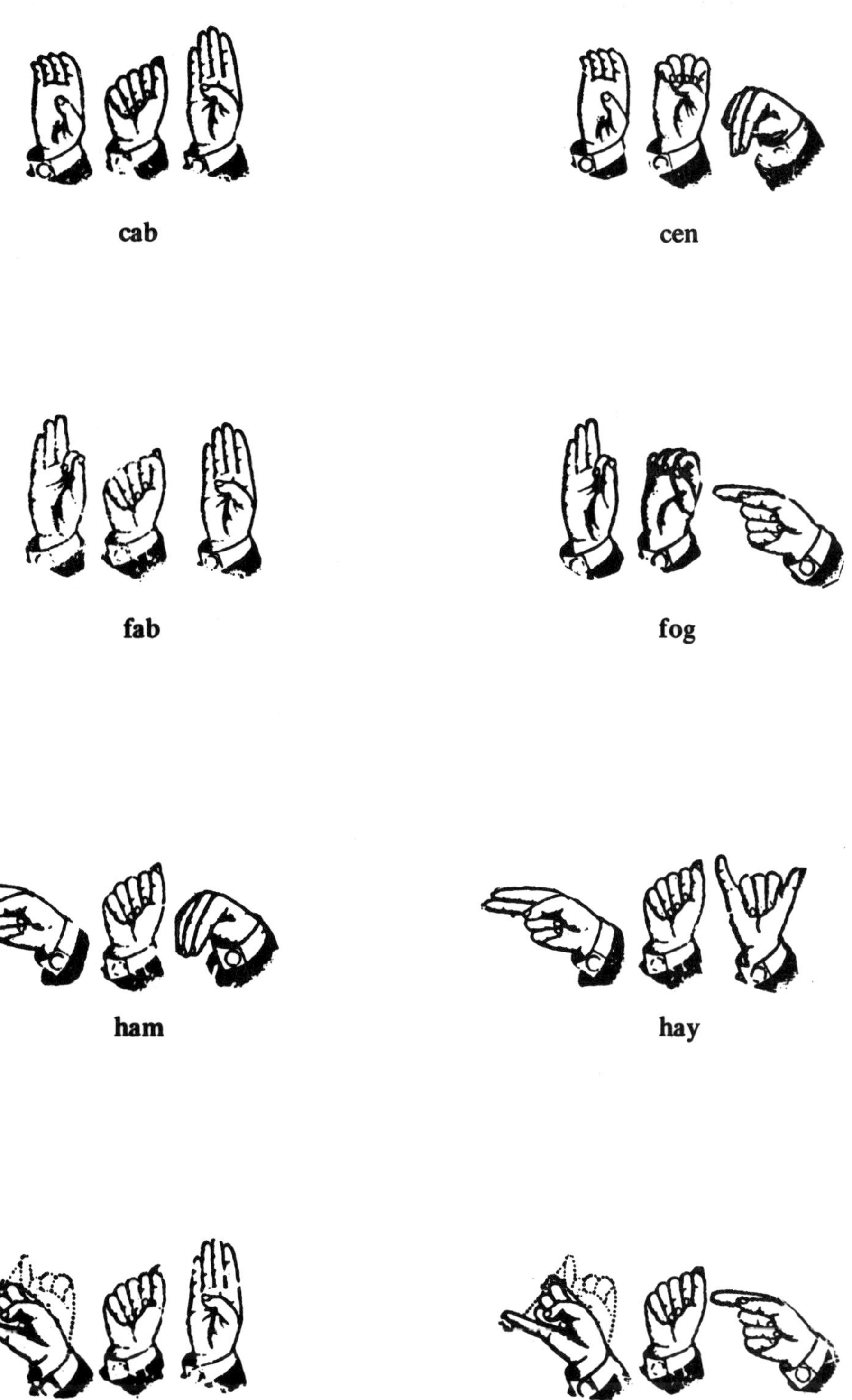
cab
cen
fab
fog
ham
hay
jab
jag

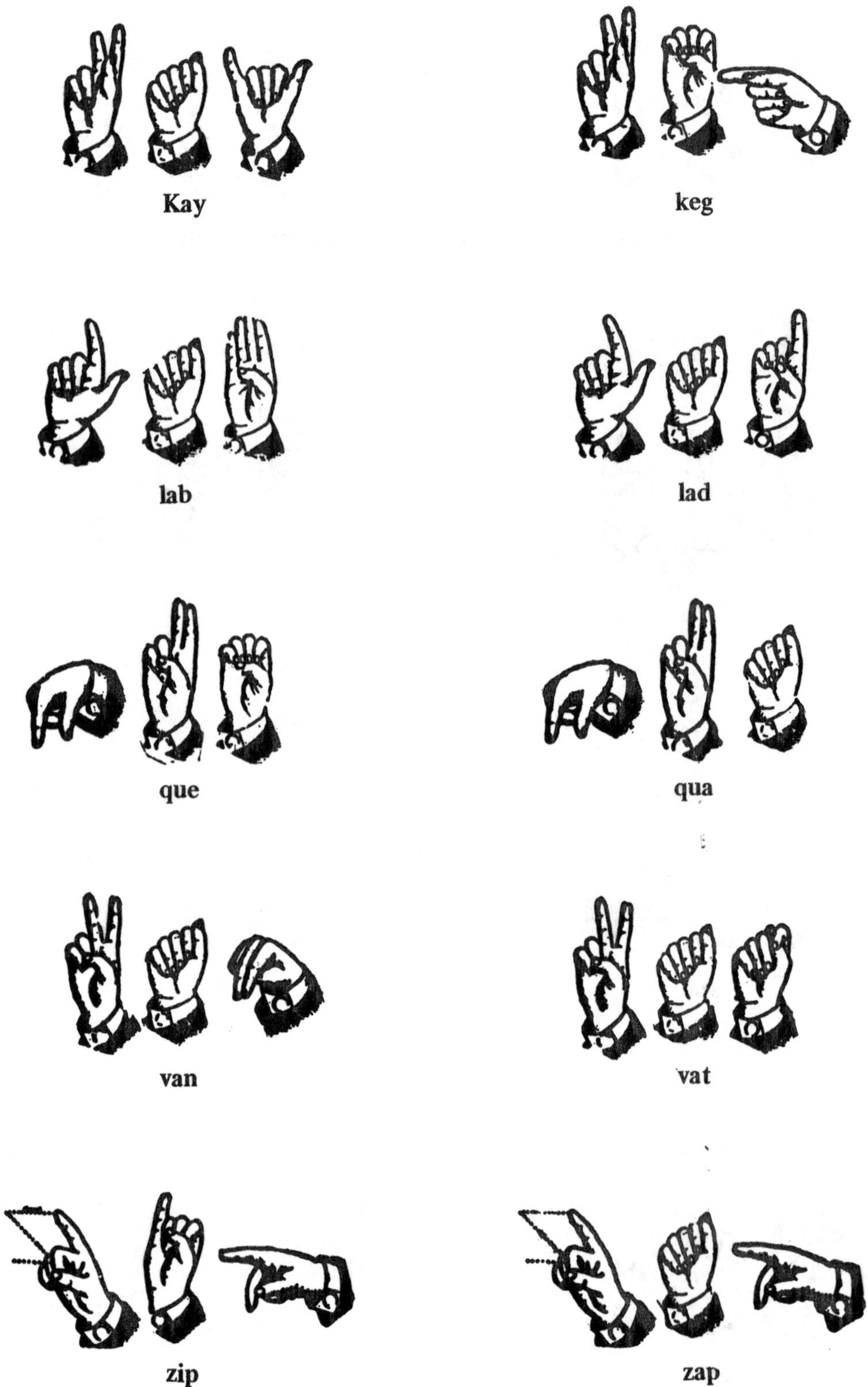
Kay
keg
lab
lad
que
qua
van
vat
zip
zap

Drills for three letter words

ab	ad	ag	am	an	ay	ap	ar
cab	dad	bag	bam	ban	bay	cap	bar
dab	fad	fag	cam	can	day	gap	car
fab	had	hag	dam	dan	fay	lap	ear
gab	lad	jag	ham	Fan	gay	map	far
jab	mad	lag	jam	man	hay	nap	jar
lab	pad	nag	lam	pan	jay	rap	mar
nab	sad	rag	mam	ran	Kay	sap	oar
tab	tad	sag	pam	san	lay	tap	par
	wad	tag	ram	tan	may		tar
		wag	sam	van	nay		war
			tam	wan	pay		
			yam		ray		
					say		

as	ax	at	ed	ee	eg	em	en
gas	jax	bat	fed	bee	beg	gem	den
has	lax	cat	led	fee	keg	hem	hen
was	tax	eat	Ned	gee	leg		men
	wax	fat	red	lee	Meg		pen
		hat	Ted	see	peg		ten
		mat	wed	tee			yen
		oat		wee			
		pat					
		rat					
		sat					
		vat					

er	et	ew	ib	id	ie	ig	im
her	bet	dew	bib	bid	die	big	aim
per	get	few	fib	did	lie	dig	dim
	jet	hew	jib	hid	pie	fig	him
	let	new	rib	kid	tie	pig	rim
	met	pew		lid	vie	rig	Tim
	net	sew		mid		wig	vim
	pet			rid			
	set						
	wet						
	yet						

is	it	in	ip	ir	ob	od	oe
his	bit	bin	dip	fir	bob	bod	doe
sis	fit	din	hip	sir	cob	God	foe
	hit	fin	lip		fob	hod	hoe
	kit	gin	nip		job	nod	Joe
	lit	pin	pip		mob	pod	toe
	mit	tin	rip		rob	rod	woe
	pit	win	sip		sob	sod	
	rit		tip				
	sit		zip				
	wit						

og	or	ot	ow	ox	ue	ub	ud
bog	for	cot	bow	box	cue	cub	bud
cog		dot	cow	fox	due	dub	cud
dog		got	how		hue	hub	mud
fog		hot	mow		rue	pub	sud
hog		jot	now		sue	rub	
jog		lot	row			sub	
log		not	sow			tub	
tog		pot	tow				
		rot					

um	on	ug	un	up	ur	us	ut
bum	bon	bug	bun	cup	bur	bus	but
gum	hon	dug	cun	pup	cur	cus	cut
hum	mon	hug	fun	sup	fur	jus	gut
mum	non	jug	gun		our	ous	hut
rum	ron	lug	hun		sur	sus	jut
sum	son	mug	jun				mut
	ton	rug	nun				nut
	won	tug	pun				out
	yon		run				put
	zon		sun				rut
							tut

Practice in Sentence Form

A few pages of nonsensical sentences using words from the previous three-letter-word practice list were used for the introduction of sentences. These may be used for practice and/or the pupils may be assigned the task of making their own sentences to be used for practice at the next class session.

The same procedure may be repeated after each practice of a new group of words.

1. Ray may pay Kay to say nay.
2. The war may mar the car.
3. Pam may nag to get a new rag.
4. The big wig was red in hue.
5. Dan had a fan in the tan van.
6. The fat cat sat in the vat and ate the rat.
7. Ted and Ned led.
8. The gas has tax.
9. The bug dug and cut a rug.
10. The pup will sup out of the cup.
11. The rod dug the sod for the hod.
12. The hen had a yen for a den in the pen.
13. Joe hit his toe on the hoe.
14. The sod was like new in the dew.
15. Sam dug the sod to get a yam.
16. Dot did not put the pot in the tub.
17. Meg can put the tee for a fee.
18. The yam was in the bag in the cab.
19. The car is red.
20. The car was big.
21. The pig had a nap.
22. The man was mad.
23. The boy was sad.
24. The dog bit his toe.
25. Woe is Joe!
26. The cue was due.
27. Ten men saw a pin.
28. How now old cow?
29. His son had fun.
30. The sap ran out.
31. The pub has Jax.
32. The fox was in a box.

DRILLS FOR FOUR-LETTER WORDS

eat	eap	ear	ean	are	een	eet	own
beat	heap	bear	bean	bare	been	beet	down
feat	leap	dear	mean	care	seen	feet	gown
heat	reap	fear	wean	dare	teen	meet	
meat		gear		fare			
neat		hear		hare			
		lear		mare			
		near		pare			
		rear		rare			
		sear		ware			
		tear					
		wear					
		year					

ope	ake	alk	ink	ock	ing	ite	ome
cope	bake	balk	link	cock	bing	bite	come
dope	cake	calk	mink	dock	ding	cite	dome
hope	fake	talk	pink	lock	king	kite	home
lope	lake	walk	rink	mock	ping	mite	some
mope	make		sink	rock	sing		
rope	rake		wink	tock	wing		
	sake			sock	zing		
	take						
	wake						

ill	elt	all	ang	ent	eak	eam	eep
fill	belt	ball	bang	bent	beak	beam	beep
gill	felt	call	fang	cent	leak	ream	deep
hill	melt	fall	gang	dent	peak	seam	keep
kill	pelt	gall	hang	gent	reak	team	peep
mill	welt	hall	pang	lent	weak		seep
pill			rang	pent			
sill			sang	rent			
will				sent			
				tent			
				vent			
				went			

one	ash	ate	ore	ent	ine	ast	ane
done	bash	bate	bore	bent	dine	cast	bane
lone	cash	date	core	cent	fine	fast	cane
bone	dash	fate	fore	dent	line	last	lane
gone	lash	gate	lore	gent	mine	mast	mane
none	mash	hate	more	pent	pine	past	pane
pone	rash	late	pore	rent	tine	vast	sane
tone	sash	mate	sore	sent	vine		vane
zone		rate	tore	tent	wine		

oat	alt	ote	ank	and	ack
boat	halt	dote	bank	band	back
coat	malt	note	lank	land	lack
goat	salt	rote	rank	sand	pack
moat		tote	sank	wand	rack
		vote	tank		tack

The mast on the boat was gone.

We will dine at the last meal.

I sent more sacks back.

The goat tore my mink.

The rate was one cent.

Neat teams line the zones.

The vane on the barn was bent.

Fill the wall vent with peat.

The zone line was past my lane.

I will be with you in a wink.

He put the sock in his shoe.

The beam was weak.

The vine was on the wall.

The gang sent meat to the king.

The gent wore a pink coat.

This year is a leap year.

He must pay more rent.

The tine of the fork was bent.

Most of the cash was mine.

The pine was near the lake.

None were left; all were gone.

The goat was lame and old.

Pack your coat in the rack.

Come down the vast hall.

The bell on the hill rang at noon.

The pool was deep and cool.

Hang your coat in the hall.

The seam in the gown was torn.

He felt a pang of fear.

Put salt on the meat.

Some had gone home.

The belt will make her gown look neat.

The boat will sink in the lake.

Dash fast to the gate.

The door was back of the sink.

He will walk and his feet will be sore.

For her sake I hope she can stay near.

She will work to make a good team.

I can hear the bell ring.

The kite will fall if we have no wind.

Her home is for rent.

This heat is more than I can bear.

They will keep land for a home site.

The gang will kill the bear.

It was a ping pong ball.

Keep the heat down low.

They sent more cash to the bank.

We will dine in that room.

We cut down the pine tree.

The mare had a long mane.

The line will move fast.

He can play with the toy boat in the sink.

Now is the time to vote.

It is past time to go.

The tank was near the sink.

The boat sank from view.

The rope had a kink in it.

The hare had seen the dog.

Why do you mope and drag your feet?

Commonly Used Words

a
an
the

as
if
for

I
he
you
we
they
it

them
us
me

our
ours
your
yours
his
her
hers
my
mine
their
its

am
are
is
do
did
doing
may
can
will
not
have
has
had
go
gone
going

or
and
because

also
too

where
how
what
when
why

reason
lesson
pupil
school

Complimentary or Courtesies

Your ____________________ is pretty.

dress
coat
hair
suit
shirt

I like your ____________________

ring
glasses
tie
shoes
watch

You look well today!

Wow! A new hairdo!

Come in.

May I help you?

Please have a seat.

Thank you.

You are welcome.

Will you help me?

Come again.

QUESTIONS

Did you have a good ____________________?

time
vacation
breakfast, dinner, supper
nap

Are you going ____________________? When?

home
to town
to the football game
to the movies

Did you go ______________________? When?

home
to town
to the football game
to the movies

WEATHER

It is ___________________________ today.

It is hot today.

cold
cool
humid
warm
cloudy
chilly

It was _________________________ yesterday.

It is a _________________________ day.

pretty
gloomy
dark
lovely
beautiful

Salutations and Answers

Hello
Good morning (afternoon, evening)
Good-by
How are you?
I am fine.
Hi

Short to long

A words

ab	ad	ag	am	an	ai	ap
cabin	fade	jagged	came	bane	baid	cape
dabbed	lade	nagged	dame	can	laid	grape
fabric	made	lagged	hammed	mane	maid	mapped
gable	paddle	rage	jammed	pane	paid	napped
lable	sadden	ragged	lame	rant	raid	rapped
table	saddle	sage	tame	sane	said	sapped
	wade	sagged		tanned		tapped
		wagged		vane		tape
		wage		wane		

ar	as	ax	at
bare	gasp	taxed	bate
care	wasp	taxi	batch
fare	hasp	waxed	cattle
jarred		waxy	eaten
marred			fatten
mare			fate
pare			hate
parred			mate
tary			pate
tarred			rate
warred			sate
ware			

E words

ed	ee	eg	em	en	er	et
redden	been	begged	gemmed	dent	herd	better
wedded	feed	legged	hemmed	henna	pert	letter
	leek	pegged		mend		meter
	seek			pend		netted
	seen			pent		petted
	teed			tend		settle
	weed			tent		wetter
						wetted

ew
dewy
hewed
newt
sewer
sewn
sewage

Short to long

i words

ie	ir	is	ib	ig	im	id	in
diet	fire	kiss	Bible	figger	aimless	bide	bind
lied	sire	sissy	fiber	digger	dime	hide	dine
pied		sister	jibe		dimmer	wide	find
tied			ribbon		dimmest	ride	pine
vied					himself		tine
					rime		wine
					time		

ip	it
pipe	bite
ripe	kite
dipped	mite
nipped	site
ripped	
sipped	

o words

ob	od	oe	og	ot	ow	ox	or
mobbed	node	does	bogged	cotton	bowed	boxed	fore
robbed	bode	doer	fogged	dotted	mowed	foxed	
sobbed	rode	toed	hogged	gotten	rowed		
			jogged	bottle	sowed		
			togged	jotted	towed		
				note			
				potted			
				rotten			

u words

ue	ub	ud	um	on	ug	un	up
cued	cube	budded	bummed	bone	buggy	bunt	cupped
duet	tube	cuddle	gummed	hone	huge	hunt	supped
hued	dubbed	muddle	humble	none	juggle	punt	
rued	rubber	sudden	mumble	tone	tugged	runt	
suet	rubbed		rumble	honey	tugger	sunny	
sued			summed			cunning	
suede						puny	

ut	ur	us
cute	cure	bust
jute	sure	just
mute	curry	oust
button	curve	usurp
cutter	burst	
gutted	surrey	

The huge dog got the bone.

We felt a sudden jolt.

The boat jammed the dock.

He went into a rage.

The wage rate was good.

We must fatten the puny runt.

A man tends the herd of cattle.

His wage made him better paid.

The man heaved the log.

Do not tarry!

The pert tot was cute.

The sunny day will redden the skin

He got a new saddle for the mare.

The maid will mend and hem the dress.

She petted the dog and he wagged his tail.

She has sewn the fabric.

The cat napped in the sun.

The cape was made of silk.

We begged her to stay.

She rubbed cotton on.

He said the bill was paid.

The taxi meter billed the fare.

The tame bear supped honey.

The cute kid sat down.

She put sage in the food.

The maid will tend the baby.

He lied and was sued for it.

The sunny surrey was not a buggy.

My cute sister cuddled the bear.

The hotter the sun, the bigger the burn.

The cunning duet robbed the tent.

All of a sudden the rumble of the surf was cut off.

The fire gutted the cabin.

We will oust the mob.

The rubber bone rocked in an aimless way.

He had just put a new gable on the cabin.

The rubber tube had no tone.

She jotted the note on a pad.

The goat nipped at the kite.

Digraphs

Two letters combined to represent one sound

wh	ch	em	fr	tr	sw
th	sl	gl	gr	st	tw
sh	ph	nk	pl	fl	sm
br	cl	bl	pr	sp	
cr	dr	dw	sk		

Digraph Words

wh	th	sh	br	cr
when	the	ship	brown	creep
what	then	shall	brush	crawl
where	than	shake	broil	cradle
why	thing	sheep	brew	crash
whale	thin	shack	breed	crept
while	that	share	bream	crain
white	then	shell	brine	cream
wheel	they	shape	brisk	creek
when	this	sharp	brior	cringe
which	throat	shave	bracket	crab
whisper	thunder	shawl	brave	crazy

ch	sl	ph	cl	dr
chair	slip	phone	clear	draw
chap	slap	photo	cloud	dry
chain	slide	pharynx	clown	drip
choke	slur	phonetics	clap	drawn
chop	slosh	phosphate	clip	drizzle
chill	sleep	phrase	clock	drab
chum	slept	physical	close	drop
chow	slight	physics	clans	drug
chore	slumber	phlox	class	drown
cheer	slim	physician	claw	drum
cheap			clean	drink

pr

prize
preen
pride
primp
prod
prattle
pray
prayer
prom

sk

skate
skip
sky
skin
skill
skirt
skit
skull
skid
ski
skim

tr

try
trip
tray
trim
trawl
trust
trial
troll
trolly
trend
travel

st

stay
stem
steer
street
strip
steed
sting
stung
stout
style
strut

fl

fly
flirt
fling
flip
flag
flour
flop
flesh
flee
flame
flat

sp

spell
spurt
spear
spurn
sport
spring
spry
sprout
speak
speed
spool

sw

sway
swat
swing
swear
swim
swam
sweet
sell
swollen
sweep
swift

tw

tweed
twice
twig
twist
twin
twelve
tweezers
twine
twitch
twitter
twilight

sm

smear
small
smart
smile
smut
smack
smug
smooth
smoke
smuggle
smock

sc

school
scream
scrap
script
scrawl
scurry
scold
scout
scoot
scoop
scorn

ea

beach
reach
teach
each
early
earn
earth
mean
lean
bean

gl

glass
glare
glean
glint
glaze
glimmer
glory
gland
glum
gleam
glue

nk

think
blink
rink
kink
link
mink
pink
sink
stink
dunk
rank

bl

black
blur
blimp
blot
blast
blink
bleed
bled
blood
bleek
block

dw

dwell
dwindle
dwarf
dwelt
dweller

fr

fry
fringe
frail
freeze
frozen
free
frost
fruit
frog
frail
fret

gr

grease
grip
green
grill
gray
gripe
graft
grab
grin
grapes
greet

pl

plead
pleat
plenty
plastic
plot
plate
plant
platter
please
plight
plaid

PREFIXES, SUFFIXES, SYLLABICATION

Prefixes

de	dis	en	ex	con
defeat	disown	enjoy	exact	concur
detour	disobey	enlist	exceed	concede
deform	disagree	enact	excite	conclude
decade	dislike	enroll	excuse	confuse
demerit	disloyal	entitle	exhale	conform

com	in	pro	re	un
complete	inhale	procede	recall	unable
comply	inside	project	renew	unfit
combine	indent	program	remake	untrue
compound	incorrect	produce	reopen	unlace
compact	informal	prolong	refresh	unpack

pre
preview
precede
prepay
prewar
prepaid

Suffixes

al	ance	able	ive	ful
postal	allowance	suitable	active	careful
optical	assistance	portable	detective	handful
critical	acquaintance	available	defective	painful
comical	disturbance	payable	destructive	joyful
personal	appearance	obtainable	excessive	helpful

y	tion	ing	ment	less
airy	action	being	payment	careless
rainy	adoption	ending	amazement	useless
rocky	edition	going	excitement	worthless
sleepy	election	earning	employment	helpless
frosty	direction	feeling	pavement	fearless

ness	ly	ous
blindness	sickly	joyous
darkness	kindly	dangerous
likeness	yearly	perilous
sadness	costly	poisonous
goodness	lively	pompous

SYLLABICATION

Compounds

air/port	ev/ery/one	ash/tray
fire/man	bed/room	af/ter/noon
pea/nut	school/room	pan/cake
hard/sh/ip	foot/st/ep	bon/fire
sun/sh/ine	un/der/st/and	bl/ue/bird

With prefixes and suffixes

con/sid/er	un/like/ly	re/cove/ry
ex/pir/ed	de/tain/ed	con/vic/tion
re/mem/ber	en/joy/ment	un/hap/py
pro/tec/tion	re/ten/tion	ex/act/ly
pro/fess/ion	con/fess/ed	in/ten/tion

The manuel alphabet is included in this booklet for purposes of reference and clarity only. It is not to be studied in alphabetical order.

The American Manual Alphabet.

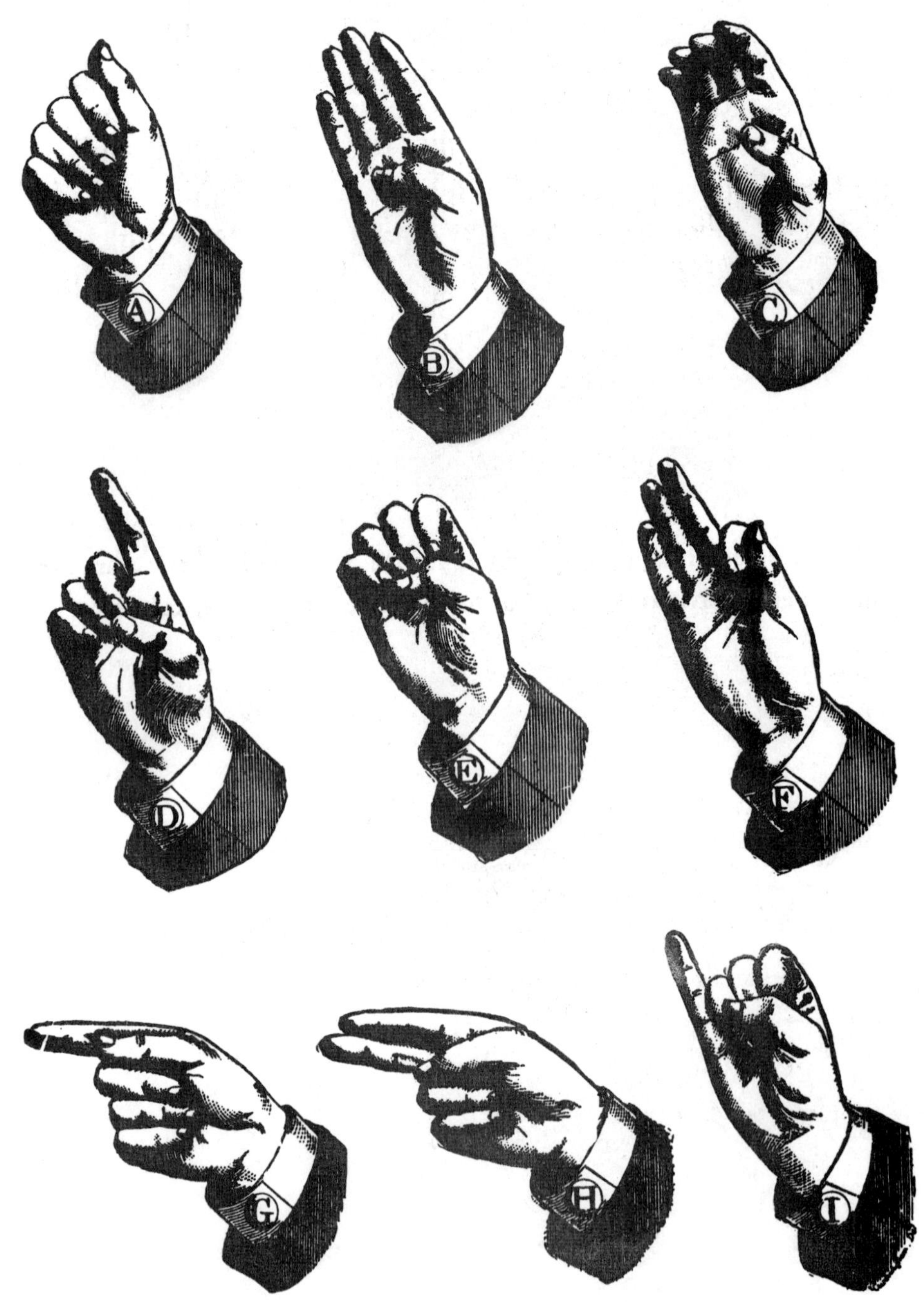

The American Manual Alphabet.

The engravings were made from photographs subjected to competent criticism, for a work on the Manual Alphabet by Prof. Joseph C. Gordon, M. A., of the Deaf-Mute College, at Washington, published by Brentano Brothers, in 1886.

The American Manual Alphabet.

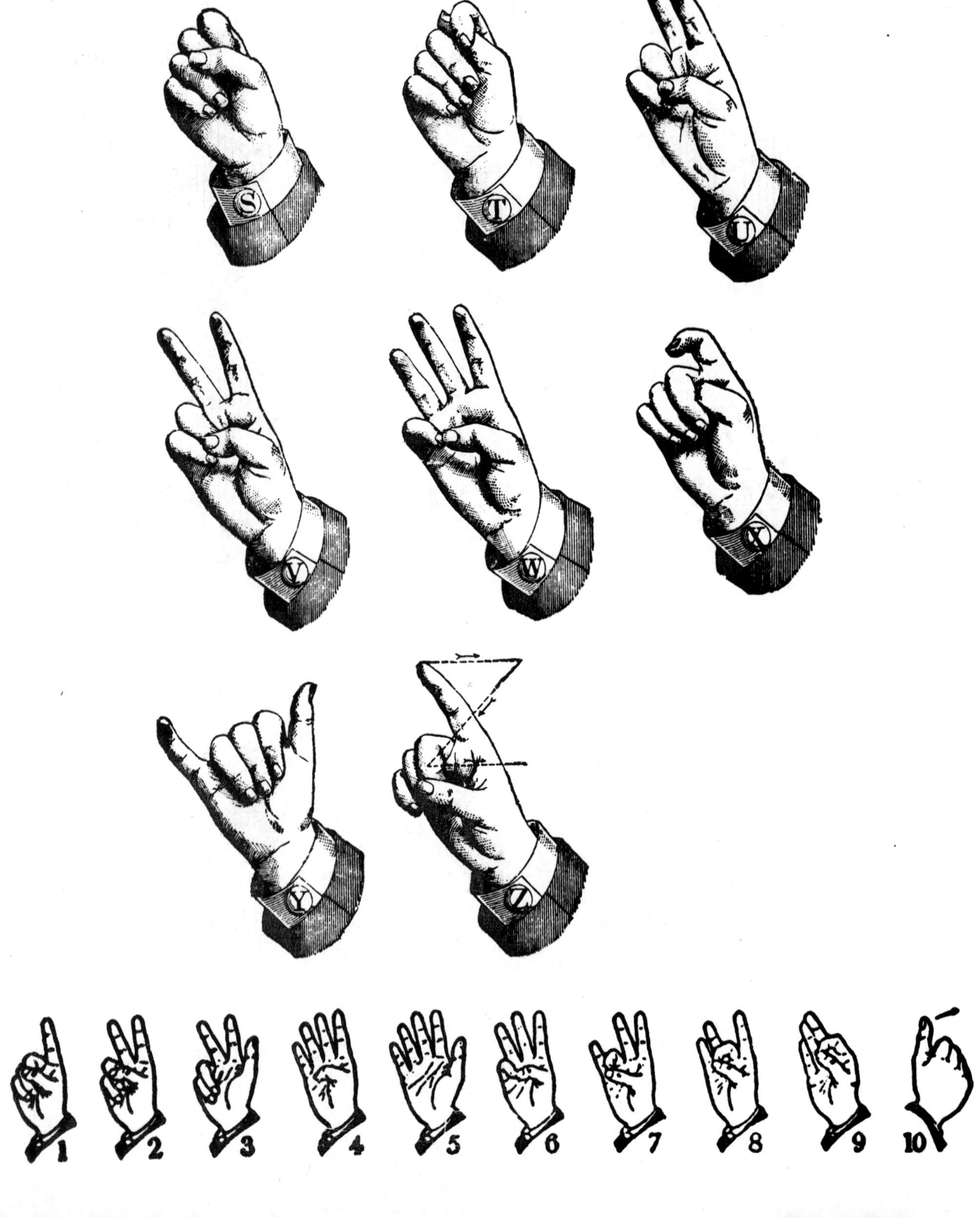